BE A GREAT THINKER

Book 3

Plato: The Father of Western Philosophy

A Young Adult's Introduction

Adrienne Roth

Matthew Roth

CONTENTS

ACKNOWLEDGMENTS

Book Cover created by Mahabuba Akter

1

SO, WHO WAS PLATO?

"All of Western Philosophy is but a footnote to Plato."

-Alfred North Whitehead, Philosopher & Mathematician

By all measures, Plato is considered one of the most influential philosophers. His works are the best known and most widely read and disseminated by western society. His impact on philosophy, science, mathematics, and critical thinking is profound.

Plato was a student of Socrates, and he was the teacher of the great philosopher Aristotle. He wrote most of his works in the form of dialogues. In these dialogues, he introduced the world to Socrates as Socrates was the main protagonist.

By the middle of Plato's life, he wrote his most famous work *Republic*, reflecting his thoughts on ethics, morals, psychology, politics, death, metaphysics, and epistemology. Epistemology is the study of knowledge. In *Republic*, Plato established his most well-known theory, the Theory of Forms.

Plato also created the idea of "platonic love," which expressed an idealized form of love that is part of longing and beauty. He conceived this kind of love as one that transcends attraction of the body and is more a union of souls.

There is some speculation, even controversy, about the chronology of when Plato's works were written. As these are ancient texts, it is sometimes hard to determine the timeline of his dialogues, for he did not date them. The task was left to historians to piece together his life and work. Over the years, some texts attributed to Plato were eventually discovered not genuine. But the work that remains is influential and is essential in studying philosophy and critical thinking.

We will review Plato's life, work, philosophies, and impact in this book. Some of his ideas might confound you, surprise you, and even inspire you. But all will show you a new way to think about the world.

2

A VERY BRIEF BIOGRAPHY OF PLATO

There is not a lot that is known about Plato's early life. Historians aren't even sure of the exact date he was born. It is accepted that he was born between 429 and 423 B.C., sometime after the Peloponnesian War. There is also some dispute from historians about where exactly he was born. Some historians believe it could have been in Athens, while others think it was Aegina.

POSEIDON

Both Plato's parents were very wealthy. They were considered aristocrats and were influential in Athens's politics and society. His father was Ariston, and his mother was Pericitone. Both sides of Plato's family claimed to trace their lineage to the God Poseidon.

It was not an uncommon practice for the aristocrats of Athens to trace their ancestry to a particular God. It was similar, in many ways, to being part of a specific sect of the religion.

Plato's real name was Aristocles, and his nickname was given to him by a relative, which indicated his size and physical prowess. The word Plato is the term for "broad," and the nickname stuck with him for his entire life.

Plato had two brothers and a sister. Plato's father, Ariston, died when Plato was a boy. His mother remarried shortly after his father's death. His stepfather was Pyrilampes, another aristocrat who advocated Athenian Democracy and was the Ambassador to Persia. Plato often looked back at his childhood with fondness. He reflected on his happy memories in his writings. Plato was a very bright student. His parents paid to get the best education for him and his siblings, including studying grammar, music, and gymnastics. He was taught by some of the most distinguished teachers of Athens society.

Early in his life, Plato took an interest in playwriting and politics. He also followed the works of Philosophers like Heraclitan and Pythagoras, which gave him knowledge of mathematics and other concepts like epistemology. He contemplated following in his stepfather's footsteps and becoming a politician but ultimately chose not to follow that path.

But the most significant influence on Plato's life came after he turned twenty and became one of Socrates' students. Socrates had such an immense impact on Plato that it completely changed the direction of his life. Following in the footsteps of Socrates, Plato devoted his life to practicing philosophy. This decision would ultimately change not only his life but sparked millennia of philosophical practice.

Plato was seriously affected by what he felt was Socrates' unfair trial and death sentence. It is partly why he started writing dialogues, using Socrates as the main character of those dialogues. He wanted to impart to the world the teachings and philosophy of Socrates.

He was so affected by Socrates' death that he spent the next 12 years traveling throughout the region, going to Sicily and Egypt, studying with other  philosophers, taking in their ideas, and creating his concepts. His Theory of Forms (which we will review later in this book) developed metaphysics and was influenced by Parmenides and Zeno of Elea. These two philosophers also appear in his dialogue, "The Parmenides."

In Plato's later life, he once again entered politics. He took a few trips to Syracuse, which was ruled by Dionysius, a very paranoid tyrant (known as the Tyrant of Syracuse). Dionysius' brother-in-law Dion was a disciple of Plato. Plato and Dion became lifelong friends. His close connection to Dion brought him to the attention of Dionysius. Plato thought he could positively influence the tyrannical leader by introducing him to philosophy. He hoped he could show Dionysius how to be a kinder leader, where he would strive to bring justice and happiness to the people of Syracuse, but this backfired.

Dionysius had a reputation for cruelty and evil. Plato's high-minded ideals soon clashed with the political realities that were part of life in Sicily. Dionysius' court was filled with suspicion and violence against objectors. He was a paranoid leader who did not trust anyone. He even killed a Captain in his army just because he had a dream about being killed by the captain. No one was safe from his paranoid delusions. Because of Dionysius's paranoia and cruelty, Plato's efforts to reform him did not work.

Plato criticized Dionysius' pleasure-seeking lifestyle. He told Dionysius that this kind of life would only lead to ruin. Not appreciating Plato's criticism and unwelcome ideas, Dionysius sold Plato into slavery. Dionysius figured in his twisted way that Plato would feel indifferent to his enslavement because Plato believed he had a righteous soul and that being a slave would not mean anything to the sanctimonious philosopher.

Fortunately for Plato, he was saved from this fate when his friends paid for his freedom. Despite this event, Plato returned a few more times to Syracuse, still attempting to change Dionysius with the help of Dion, but it never worked. Dionysius did not try to sell Plato into slavery again on the bright side. Some historians think this incident was the main reason Plato decided to return to Athens.

Plato returned to Athens from his travels around 387 B.C. when he was around 40 years old. He founded a new philosophical school named after the Greek god Academes and called it the Academy. He placed this state-of-the-art school just outside the city walls of Athens. It was an open-air campus.

At the Academy, Plato delivered lectures and taught various philosophical subjects to the brightest students. These students came from all over the Greek world to study with him. One of his most famous students, Aristotle, arrived at the Academy at age seventeen. Aristotle remained at the Academy, learning, and teaching there for over 20 years. Aristotle differed in his philosophies from his teacher Plato in that his ideas were more grounded in science, while Plato's view of the world was more abstract.

It is believed that most of Plato's dialogues were written during the years that Plato taught and ran the Academy.

Plato died around the age of 81. Much like the speculation on his birth, there are various ideas about how he died. Some say he died at a wedding feast; others say Plato was lying on his deathbed, being serenaded by a flute that a young girl played. Others say he died a simple, unexciting death, alone in bed. Most historians believe he was buried where his Academy once stood.

Plato's work would inspire western societies with his philosophies, creating a new way to look at life, love, and the physical world. In his words and dialogues, we discover these incredible concepts. For these reasons, Plato is considered the Father of Western Philosophy.

3

IT WAS PLATO WHO INTRODUCED THE WORLD TO SOCRATES.

One of Plato's accomplishments was to bring the world the philosophies of his beloved teacher, Socrates. That being said, much of what we know and understand about Socrates comes from the dialogues written by Plato and not directly from Socrates, as the master and teacher never wrote any of his philosophies down.

Socrates was a much older, wiser man than Plato, and Socrates changed how Plato viewed the world. Plato elevated Socrates in the many dialogues he wrote.

In his early years, Plato was mainly influenced by presocratic thinkers, who based their thought process on high-minded ideals such as metaphysics and epistemology. This early influence did rule some of Plato's later works and was the basis for the Theory of Forms. But it was Socrates that laid the fundamental foundation for how Plato would lead his life, teaching him how to think critically and how to maintain a virtuous life.

At first, Plato considered a life in politics, much like his ancestors. But after watching the trial and ultimate death sentence of his beloved teacher, he became disillusioned with politics and chose to live his life by writing and teaching philosophy. It was the best decision he could have made, for if he had decided to go into politics, he probably would have drifted into obscurity. The Western world would never have experienced his concepts, and the world would have been different without his influence.

It was Plato that introduced the Socratic Method. And Plato's early dialogues reflected mainly on Socrates and his philosophies.

In Plato's later dialogues, he wrote about Socrates' defense at his trial in 399 B.C. Plato wrote what he attributed were Socrates' thoughts as he contemplated his life and his death, preparing to drink the deadly hemlock. However, many people believe that Plato skimmed over the real reasons Socrates was put on trial and found guilty. Plato's exclusion of this truth was mainly due to his high regard for Socrates. He did not want to mar his beloved teacher's memory. Plato did marvel at how Socrates handled himself throughout his trial, how Socrates accepted his death sentence, and how he refused to take the opportunity to escape that sentence. Plato was quite affected by his teacher's internal strength in facing such a terrible consequence.

Plato, who wrote as Socrates, showed the world how to accept the limits of humanity and how humans need to develop knowledge and wisdom by breaking down and finding the root of all arguments through questions and contemplations. Plato truly felt that Socrates was a messenger from the Gods. Although Socrates likely would not have agreed with Plato's assessment of him in this regard. Plato reflected on Socrates' modesty and humility that he was an ordinary man who embraced uncertainty and doubt.

We need to thank Plato for bringing these concepts to the world and using Socrates as the main protagonist of these dialogues. The words attributed to Socrates have helped others develop their critical thinking skills and advanced western philosophy to a place of high regard.

4

PLATO'S VIEW OF KNOWLEDGE

"If a man neglects education, he walks lame to the end of his life."

- Plato

Plato often used Socrates as a mediator to present his concepts and ideas. When doing so, Plato established his thought process by utilizing stories or allegories inspired by these Socratic concepts.

One of Plato's more complex theories was his Theory of Knowledge. This theory requires much contemplation and introspection upon its review, and most people, regardless of their age or interest in philosophy, have a hard time understanding it completely.

In Plato's opinion, knowledge and education went hand in hand. He wrote in one dialogue that Socrates felt knowledge was the basis of virtue. By being educated, we can achieve justice, both socially and individually. Once we educate ourselves on how people from various societies and cultures live, who they are, and how they behave, we can understand them better. By understanding them, we can relate to them, and they are no longer a mystery. We realize they are like us. When we form this kind of knowledge of others, we can act with more justice. By developing our sense of justice, we then achieve excellence. For the ancient Greeks, excellence was a virtue.

Plato felt that knowledge was attainable to all who sought it. He thought that knowledge needed to be infallible and based on reality. The truth was objective, and it comes from beliefs that, put to the test, do not crumble on inspection.  These beliefs must be tethered to reality, and truth must come from logical reasoning. The facts must be supported by deep thought - introspection, and evidence. Plato felt knowledge was buried deep into a person's subconscious. We, as human beings, understand things intuitively, like beauty, justice, and equality. It is inherent in a person's psyche.

Plato concluded that social justice could only be achieved when all social classes, whether workers or leaders, rich or poor, male or female, young or old, live together in a harmonious state. He believed that all people could exist together when society gave them the same educational and economic opportunities. If all people cannot be given equal education, starting from an early age, they will never be able to compete, and there will not be a fair playing field. Plato felt that unequal education would lead to an unjust society. And Plato argued that an unfair society leads to political systems run by tyrants, oligarchs, and unqualified individuals who create totalitarian regimes and defective democracies.

Many societies thought there was little correlation between economics and education. Those who felt this way put businesses in charge of the education system, which was done when Plato lived. Plato was in complete disagreement with having business tied to education. He felt that trade and commerce were too interested in making profits rather than challenging and developing minds to think critically. These business influences also tended to play the education system unfairly, giving help to one class of people above another. Plato believed that proper and good education should have no attachment to private enterprise and profit-making. The best, honest and uncorrupted education was only concerned with the common good and was based on human principles and social justice.

Plato created four stages in the development of Knowledge. These stages are Plato's Theory of Knowledge or Plato's epistemology.

The first stage in Plato's theory was **Imagining**.

Now, Plato did not wholly respect imagination. He felt imagination was an illusion of "true reality." Imagination was more like a shadow of the natural world than the real world itself. He felt imagination was primarily associated with the irrational part of the human soul.

Yet, at the same time, he did feel there was an essential role in arts in our education system. Our education and knowledge development began with our imagination. Myths, stories, and poetry presented it. Our imagination helps us to attain wisdom regarding understanding humans. Our imagination can help put us into the shoes of others and thereby contribute to our social awareness. Imagination also allows us to understand philosophical and social concepts because we can imagine different scenarios. Our imagination is the steppingstone to the rest of our knowledge and development.

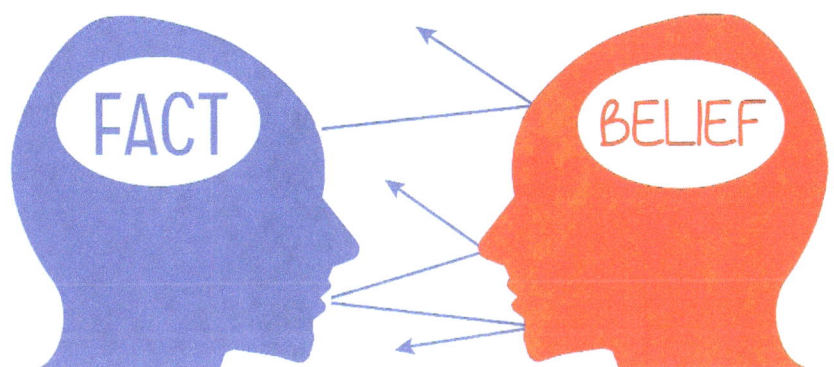

The second stage in Plato's Theory of Knowledge is **Belief.**

Plato felt that just seeing something does not necessarily mean believing in it. We must first believe that what we are witnessing is fact and is rooted in reality. We may see a shadow or an image in our imagination and conceive it as accurate, though it is still just part of our imagination. Belief takes us one step further. With belief, we start to question the shadow or the image. We begin to learn more about it through those questions. It then takes on a higher meaning or level. At this stage, we go deeper into understanding it.

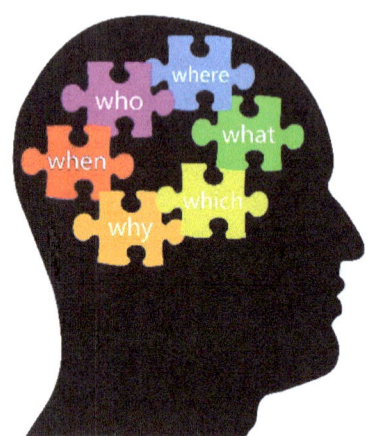

The third stage in Plato's Theory of Knowledge is **Thinking**.

In this stage in our journey into knowledge, Plato felt we move from the visible world, where we can see and touch everything, to the intelligible world. At this stage, the questions we have about the images and shadows that we see take on a more reflective meaning. We have gone from simply imagining it, questioning it, to analyzing it. In the analysis, we start to form ideas about the image. We break it down to see all the parts and pieces. This is the stage that scientists and scholars follow. At this level in the Theory of Knowledge, a person does not take anything at face value. They ask many pertinent questions, create a hypothesis, and gain more knowledge to find the answers to sometimes impossible questions. The intention is to gather as much information on an item as possible and learn about it from all sides.

The final stage in the Theory of Knowledge is **Perfect Intelligence**.

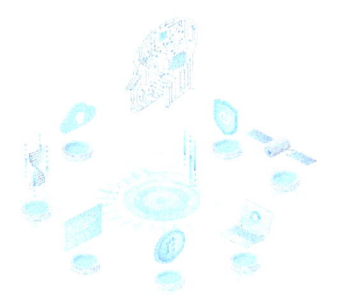

Perfect intelligence goes far beyond the realm of a hypothesis. At this point in the journey of knowledge, an individual can acquire the lowdown on a subject and apply it satisfactorily in the world. Some believe that artificial intelligence is perfect intelligence, as it is not based on imagination or belief, goes beyond hypothesis, and relies only on facts to make conclusions. Few humans can achieve perfect intelligence, as we seem to have too many roadblocks to gaining the answers and applying our knowledge in an ideal manner.

Plato's use of allegories helped to explain his concepts. We will delve further into these allegories later in this book. Plato liked to lead his students down various paths to help them answer their questions and form their ideas. Plato compared ignorance to the educated and imagination to reality. He tried to show the limitations humans have when pursuing knowledge. He aimed to continuously develop his student's learning while never succumbing to ignorance.

Do you agree with Plato that we all should have the same education, no matter who we are or what we have or don't have, or where we live?

Do you agree with Plato that we learn to have more justice only by being more educated?

Do you personally feel that you have an advantage or a disadvantage in your education?

What can you personally do to bring more justice into the world?

Which path in the journey of knowledge do you feel you are on at this point in your life?

5

PLATO'S FASCINATING THEORY OF FORMS

We are about to review a theory that some have considered controversial, confounding, and inexplicable. It is a theory that has been dissected and contemplated by scholars, philosophers, scientists, theologians, writers, and great thinkers throughout the centuries.

Imagine if everything you saw, touched, and experienced in your daily life was an illusion. That reality existed in a different realm, a place you could not see, and what you understand as "real" does not exist; it is just a shadow of the other realm. How would you feel about this? Is this something you can even contemplate?

This is what Plato conceived, to a greater degree, in his Theory of Forms.

Plato presented his Theory of Forms in his works of **Phaedo** and **Republic**. Plato conceived that there were two realms or realities where humans existed. The first is the physical realm that rules our everyday existence. It is the one you understand because you experience it first-hand. It is what you can see, taste, touch, and feel in your daily life. It is also far from being perfect.

The other realm is non-physical, more spiritual, which Plato considered perfection. He called this realm the Theory of Forms, also known as the Realm of Ideas. How Plato perceived these forms were perfect and unchanging, and often abstract. They can be aspatial or related to space; and atemporal or connected to time.

According to Plato, an aspatial form does not have a physical dimension and has no orientation in space. They do not have any particular location and can exist anywhere and do exist everywhere. Similarly, an atemporal form does not exist in time. It becomes the basis for the Theory of Time and is considered by Plato to be what time is all about. Atemporal forms are not mortal. They can live forever. They do not have a beginning or an end, and this is what Plato considered perfection.

Plato used the example of the triangle when describing his forms.

He used this example when explaining the Form of Beauty. Triangles have three sides. If you draw the triangle as a human, your illustration of that triangle will be imperfect and have flaws. But the "true" Form of the triangle, which exists beyond our realm, is ever constant and unchanging. It is precisely the same no matter who considers it. Time only affects the individual regarding the triangle, not the triangle itself, which never changes. This same attribute is thus given to all Forms within Plato's Theory of Forms.

Plato also discussed another Form as the Divine Form. These forms lack the flaws that plague humans. They belong to a higher order of existence. The concept of the soul, of a supreme being, of the basis of religious beliefs, falls into this Form. Plato's Divine Form is where the inspiration came for the Christian concept of heaven.

Then there is the final Form, which is what Plato considered imperceptible. These are forms that can be conceived of but are not seen. In his Allegory of the Caves, which Plato presented in ***Republic,*** this is what he described regarding this concept:

There is a group of prisoners chained up together in a cave. This cave is the only reality they know and understand. A light in the cave comes from a fire that burns directly behind the prisoners. The fire is used for warming the prisoners. The light from that fire is reflected on the wall of the cave.

The prisoners have a clear view of this wall, and it is the only thing that these prisoners can see. They do not have any other perception other than what is shown on the wall. Throughout the years, objects are passed in front of the fire. These objects project as shadows on that wall.

As the prisoners watch these things, they begin to have a distinct idea of what a bird, a ball, a flag, etc., looks like, but their perceptions of these items are not real. They are not based on reality, as they are merely shadows of the actual objects. In this simplified manner, Plato wanted to show in this allegory that what humans perceive as reality is not reality. He believed that only until the prisoners (aka humans) are released from their chains and see how Forms are (or what the truth is) will this be the only time humans will understand their place in the world.

The Allegory of the Caves is a concept many have used to describe their theories about "true" reality. You might recognize this allegory if you have ever heard of or watched the movie "*The Matrix*." The idea behind this movie was taken directly from Plato's allegory. It theorizes that we live in a simulation of the real world. This idea presented in "*The Matrix*"  has taken hold of our culture and psyche. It became a popular notion that we genuinely don't know if what we experience in our daily lives is real. We must seek enlightenment by the idea that there is so much more that we need to understand about our world.

Are we only experiencing shadows and not reality?

When something odd happens that is inexplicable, we now use the term "a glitch in the Matrix." It is the way we say that something in that other non-physical realm has suddenly penetrated through our physical realm. This "glitch" is the only way to perceive this odd occurrence.

Can you accept this concept? Is this something you have contemplated as well? Or does this seem like something too farfetched to believe?

Over the centuries, the Theory of Forms has been the primary basis for Metaphysical Theory and Epistemology.

Metaphysical Theory is concerned with the nature of reality. It is how humans find their place in that reality (aka *The Matrix*).

As we have stated earlier, Epistemology is the study of knowledge. It looks at what is a belief and what is an opinion. It also studies how knowledge is acquired. Plato distinguished what is actual knowledge and what is just opinion. He felt that opinions were shifting, evolving, and imperfect. They could change at the drop of a hat and be rarely solid. On the other hand, knowledge derives from timeless or aspatial Forms. Plato used this concept in the Allegory of the Caves.

The Theory of Forms also tackles moral problems. Plato believed that abstract moral concepts also had forms. These include beauty and good and evil. Evil is often debated as to what is considered evil. This isn't always black and white, and the definition in the real-world changes, so it is not perfect.

There were many criticisms of the Theory of Forms. Plato himself was aware of the problems in his Theory. He even offered those criticisms in his work, *Parmenides*. One criticism was his concept of the form of a day. He stated that a day could be everywhere and all at one time. In this regard, a day becomes a concept that is too hard to conceptualize. What is a day in the universe? What does a day mean? Plato also was unsure where the line between a Form and a non-Form is made. There were far too many questions and not enough answers or evidence.

But despite the errors and inconsistencies of the Theory of Forms, it did mark a significant advancement in Philosophy. It expressed how we view the world, what is accurate, and just a perception. It gave way to other theories such as the Big Bang Theory and the multi-verse idea, and it tackled far deeper things such as the soul and religion.

The Theory of Forms lends to the argument that people cannot accept the information presented to them as the be-all-end-all knowledge of the world. People must engage in rational thought to understand the world. But, to this day, many people do not embrace the Theory of Forms. It is a challenging idea for many to grasp. But like in the movie *The Matrix,* it had us contemplating a new idea about reality.

It is up to you to make up your mind about the relevance and the prospect of this Theory. Will the Theory of Forms concept help you view the world and your reality differently? Or is this concept just too far out of the left field to accept? Only you can determine what the correct answer is for yourself.

⚛ 6 ⚛

PLATO'S TAKE ON LOVE

"Every heart sings a song, incomplete until another heart whispers back. Those who wish to sing always find a song. At the touch of a lover, everyone becomes a poet."

- Plato, "The Symposium"

In the dialogues, *The Lysis* and *The Symposium* - Plato writes in-depth about love and friendship, or Eros and Philia.

In *The Symposium*, Plato defines Eros as two types of love – the Earthly Eros and the Divine Eros.

Earthly Eros (or Vulgar Eros) discusses attraction towards a person's beauty related to desirability. It pertains to physical pleasure and reproduction.

Divine Eros often starts as a physical attraction but develops into something beyond the physical and is more ethereal. It goes into a higher plane, is related to beauty, and is close to the divine. This divine love is known by the term "Platonic Love."

Plato never used the term, Platonic Love. The Florentine scholar Marsilio Ficino coined that term back in the 15th century.

In Plato's examination of Divine Eros, he uses a dialogue made by Socrates during a dinner party. Socrates asks each guest at the party to participate in a speech contest. Each contestant must deliver an impromptu lecture about their take on love. Each contestant has a different view on love, and these thoughts create a kind of development of love in stages. Socrates then summarizes each speech at the end of the contest, using the teachings of the prophet Diotima (who created the "science of all things relating to love.") From these speeches, he establishes the Ladder of Love.

Plato refers to this ladder in this regard: a person must understand each step as they climb this ladder, and they cannot move to the next step in the ladder without that understanding. The higher the person climbs on this ladder, the more intellectual and divine a love becomes.

We will examine these steps of love as Plato describes them in *The Symposium*.

The first step on the ladder of love is **Love for a Particular Body**.

This step pertains to a love related to an attraction a person feels towards a particular feature that another person possesses. Someone feels this attraction because they may be missing that desirable feature on their own body.

This trait can pertain to the color of a person's eyes, smile, or hairstyle; they may have dimples or a svelte body. Whatever that particular desirable feature is, this is what a person needs to feel that physical attraction.

The second step on the ladder of love is **Love for All Bodies**.

When someone who moves to this step of the ladder begins to understand what feature attracts them (pouty lips, blue eyes, a bright smile), the person on this step can appreciate this trait no matter who

possesses it. This makes it easier for a person to go beyond the superficial attraction of just one physically appealing person to become an appreciation of anyone who holds the desired traits.

The third step on the ladder of love is **Love for Souls**.

In this step, physical features are no longer critical. A person will be more interested in a person's mind, intellect, and personality. Friendship and other deeper relationships now transcend physical attraction. You begin to appreciate an enjoyable conversation with a cherished friend or classmate at this stage. You love to be in someone's company because you feel they are a kindred spirit or your intellectual equal. The thrill is just being in their presence. This position on the ladder most reflects the ideas of Platonic Love.

The fourth step on the ladder is a **Love for Laws and Institutions**.

Plato describes this step in this way: good people make good laws and good institutions.

Plato explained that people who move to this level on the ladder live by a higher moral standard. Plato believed in the goodness of humans when it came to their approach to laws and institutions. It was a bright and hopeful idea but is up for debate and contemplation.

Do you agree with Plato? Is love for your institutions and laws a higher form of love?

Should we consider this at all when we are discussing love?

Knowing about Plato's life, especially his experiences with Dionysius, how do you think this affected Plato's relationship and ideas about laws and institutions?

The fifth step on the ladder of love is **Love for Knowledge.**

This step pertains to the hunger of individuals to seek and attain knowledge in all its forms. Seeking knowledge can be as simple as reading an informational book, magazine, or newspaper article. It can be listening to a podcast or a vlog, watching a documentary, taking in a lecture from a scholar, or simply consuming everything you can on a subject to understand it completely and thoroughly. You do not need to go to the best schools to satiate this hunger and love for knowledge. Anyone can immerse themselves in this stage. This step brings you closer to the divine and puts you on a higher plane. To Plato, this stage brings a person closer to a deeper philosophical understanding of the world.

The sixth and last step on the ladder of love is **Love for Love Itself**.

Plato ascribed this step in his Theory of Forms as the Form of Beauty. In this stage, an individual on this level will see beauty as it is – without question or conditions. Love for Love itself is the love for an eternal or undefined entity. It is the ultimate stage about the highest and most complex of the steps and is up to interpretation, as people have their concepts of what the divine is and what beauty is. This love is in the eye of the beholder.

People may take it literally that it is the love for God, while others see it as a full appreciation of nature and our planet, and yet others might see it as a complete acknowledgment of science and the universe.

What someone feels is the most sacred object in their world is up to a very personal interpretation and can only be answered by each person in their way.

Looking at these steps in the ladder of love, where do you see yourself on this journey?

Have you found a friend you are close to and with whom you share a deep connection?

Do you participate in the institutions of your community or at school?

Are you actively seeking knowledge to know more about a subject you are enthusiastic about?

You do not need to follow a well-worn path in any of these. It is up to you to climb the ladder while learning to appreciate each stage as you experience them. You are on a constant path to finding the ultimate love of the divine, whatever the divine means to you.

☙ 7 ☙

PLATO'S VIEWS ON THE SOUL

"All souls are immortal. For that which is always in motion is immortal; that which moves something else and is moved by something else. In ceasing from movement ceases from living."

- **Plato**

The idea of the soul is a human concept that goes as far back as the ancient Egyptian and Chinese cultures. Each of these societies believed in a dual soul. The soul is what remains behind after the physical body departs.

The ancient Hebrews also had a concept of the soul. Only they did not believe the soul separated from the body.

Christians view the soul from ancient Greek society and Plato's Soul Theory.

In one of his Socratic dialogues and teachings, Plato wrote that Socrates felt that the psyche was the essence of a person. This essence determines how a person behaves. Plato believed that this essence was one of the most important aspects of a person's being. Plato also believed that a person's soul existed after death. He believed that even after a person dies, their soul continues to live on and is, in fact, reborn and can exist in new bodies.

Plato was the first philosopher to offer that the soul was the source of our lives and minds. He also felt our soul was the basis of our morals. Our soul is the thing that gives our body life. It rules our senses, feelings, and our entire being.

In Plato's Theory of Soul, he conceived that the soul consisted of three parts. These parts are located throughout our bodies.

The first part of the soul is the **Logos**. This part of the soul is in the head and oversees reason and logic. It helps to regulate all the other parts of the soul. It is what rules us as human beings.

The second part of the soul is the **Thymos**.

The Thymos is in the chest area. This part of the soul refers to our spirit in that it rules our emotional side and our need to fight and is what engages us in debate and

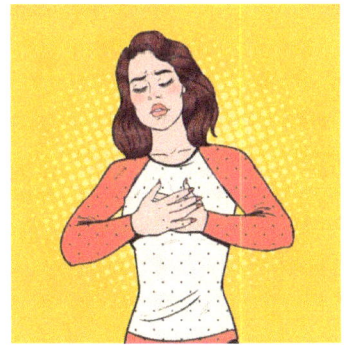

arguments. It expresses our desire to succeed and to gain recognition for our accomplishments. It is what moves us to act and to achieve.

The third part of the soul is **Eros**. This part of the soul is in the stomach region. Eros rules our desires. Eros binds us to other individuals through love, passion, friendship, and hate. It guides our emotional and creative side. Eros is the part of the soul that inspires our connection to earthly and spiritual things.

You can consider Plato's Theory of Soul in this regard: if Logos primarily rules your soul, then you are led by your head; if Thymos primarily rules your soul, then you are led by your heart; and if Eros primarily rules your soul, then you are guided by your gut.

So, which of these parts of your soul are you led by?

Like other ancient societies, Plato also conceived of reincarnation in his Theory of Soul. He did not believe that a person would be punished after death for doing terrible things but instead would return to the earth in another form – as a lesser species. It was a way to make amends for what they could not accomplish in their past life. A man, in this regard, would return to the earth as a woman. In ancient Greek society, women were considered lesser members of their culture. A woman would then return to the world as an animal. Animals would then be reborn as snakes. Snakes would be reborn as insects.

Plato asserted that the afterlife was more in line with reward and punishment, based on the person's previous life. But there is an argument from various scholars that Plato did not fully believe in this concept. Though he may have written dialogues on the idea, at the same time, his thoughts on it may have only been an allegory. The fact was that Plato did explain his concepts by writing allegories. Because of this, the Theory of Soul is much debated and up to interpretation.

On the other hand, the Christian church took Plato's word on the soul as a literal interpretation. Plato's teachings heavily influenced them. It is especially so when it comes to the concept of Heaven.

Plato wrote that when our soul is released from our imperfect body at death, it is set free. The body is a prison or tomb for the soul in Plato's view. In the end, the soul is then sent to live in the realm of pure Forms.

This idea appealed to the early fathers of the Christian Church. They were deeply influenced by Greek philosophy. They believed philosophers like Plato were imbued with divine revelation through Logos, imparting human reason and wisdom. Philosophy helped to develop the Christian Church's sense of holiness and righteousness. The famous theologian Augustine felt that only by studying Plato first was he then able to receive the gospel of the Lord. Augustine felt that once the soul leaves the body and goes into that higher realm of Forms, this brings the soul to Heaven, where the Forms exist.

The Roman Catholic Church accepted this spiritualized view of the soul, and it remains the dominant view. To some degree, Plato inspired the concept of Heaven. Whether fact or an abstract idea, Heaven is initially a Platonic concept but has been taken to another level through religious doctrine.

But remember, you are a burgeoning philosopher. You are a critical thinker. What do you feel is the concept of the soul?

Do you believe in Heaven and Hell?

What do you think happens after you die?

Do you feel the soul rules our essence?

It is interesting to speculate on this aspect of our existence and non-existence. The concept of the soul taps into the

deepest regions of your thoughts and ideas of what life and death mean.

8

BRING SOME PLATO INTO YOUR LIFE

Even though some of Plato's philosophies and concepts are complex, he did create a blueprint on how to live one's life better. Here are a few quotes and ideas of Plato that might help you view the world more succinctly.

"Opinion is the medium between knowledge and ignorance."

As Plato stated, it is okay to have an opinion, but opinions on their own need to be backed up by facts and logic. If you present an idea without correct and proven information to support that idea, then you are blowing off steam and not adding anything to the argument. This may not be a problem if the intention is to simply make noise. But if you want your opinion respected by others, you need to make a solid argument. This is the best time to show off your ability as a critical thinker.

Have you come across a situation recently where you were caught in an argument, and either you or the person you were arguing with did not have all the facts? How did you handle it?

"Knowledge becomes evil if the aim is not virtuous."

Plato thought that when you are educated, you should not use what you have learned in a way that would harm others. Plato felt very strongly that education was linked to being virtuous and was integral to a more just society. It is said that "knowledge is power." In that regard, it should be your goal in life to use your knowledge for the good of society and not take advantage of others who are less educated and, in turn, more vulnerable because of their ignorance. Being helpful to others, teaching others what you know, is truly where the power lies.

Are you good at something, such as math, English, science, music, or sports?

Does your knowledge make you feel you have a competitive advantage?

Would you be open to teaching others what you know so you could help them achieve success?

"Ignorance is the root and stem of all evil."

Though Plato felt that knowledge could sometimes be used to take advantage of others, he believed that ignorance is the main reason for bad intentions. When someone is ignorant about a subject or towards a group of people, they become scared and may lash out, which causes them to act irrationally and do harmful and hurtful things to those they don't understand and fear. To prevent being ignorant, you need to learn about those different from you. It may not be easy to immerse yourself in an idea or surround yourself with individuals who are not the same as you, but it will make you well-rounded and empathetic to those who do not share your same background or ideologies. You want to put yourself in someone else's shoes, understand how they feel, experience the world, and see if you can relate to them somehow. Only until you do this will you rid yourself of unconscious biases and become less ignorant and more informed.

Look closely at yourself. Do you think you have any unconscious bias towards others?

How do you think you can learn about others who are different from you?

Are you willing to get to know someone who does not share your same background, culture, race, or religion?

"Necessity is the mother of invention."

Plato asserted that when there is a crisis, we need to find a way to respond to it by innovating. An excellent example of this is the COVID-19 pandemic. When it started, no one had a way to stop the virus, and with people getting extremely sick and dying, there was a need to  find a way to stem the crisis. It was then that scientists and other individuals came together to figure out how to stop the spread of the virus. They worked together to create ways to block the virus by using hand sanitizers, wearing masks, and developing ground-breaking vaccines. It was something that the world did together to stop this terrible situation.

You also need to follow this Platonic idea by doing what you can to stave off a crisis in your life. Innovation is what makes us able to face challenges. We need to be creative as we embark on our personal battles. It takes some practice to do this, but if you can learn to innovate when a situation gets tough, you will be able to face any crisis head-on.

What do you do when you come across a problematic situation in your life? Do you hide from it, or do you face it head-on and find a solution to make the situation better?

Have you found yourself in a crisis where you were the one to solve the problem with your ingenuity?

"One of the penalties for refusing to participate in politics is that you end up being governed by your inferiors."

Plato said people must take a more significant role in their local, state, federal, and even school government. By doing so, a person will have more say in how they are governed. When you vote, you should not just vote during a presidential election but in every election. Each election is crucial. Electing a city councilperson, a state representative, or judges on the bench can affect your life directly or indirectly. It would help if you were educated on who is running for office, whether in your school or the local or federal government. Ask questions about who these politicians are, what they stand for, and what they don't stand for, and see if they would be helpful to the issues that are most important to you; and will be amenable to making changes in their ideas, if necessary.

Don't be charmed by slick advertisements and clever slogans; look deep into a candidate's ideology. If something doesn't seem right, don't support them. The only way you can understand this is to be more involved in politics. The worst thing for society is to have an apathetic electorate. Apathy leads to a lack of interest, and eventually, we are governed by persons who should never be in government. We give our rights to those not necessarily looking out for our best interests by being indifferent. Take an active role in politics, and then you will never give your rights away.

What issues are the most important to you right now?

Have you ever been involved in a political campaign?

Have you thought of running for office at your school?

How can you be more involved in your government so your opinion and voice count?

"Courage is knowing what not to fear."

Plato believed that even though you sometimes face something scary, you need to muster the courage to face what scares you to conquer it.

You also need to understand that sometimes fear keeps you from accomplishing something important. When this happens, we don't achieve our goals because we are afraid that something might go wrong and we will fail.

President Franklin Roosevelt famously said, "The only thing we have to fear is fear itself." He made this statement to bring hope to a scared society dealing with many complex issues. In the 1930s, when he said this, fear kept people from moving forward, and it took courage to make the extraordinary changes this country needed to lift itself out of the Great Depression. Use his words and Plato's as an example for your life.

Don't let fear rule your life. Even if it is scary to try something new, to embark on a difficult task, it takes courage to be different and try something out of your comfort zone. You can only grow as a person if you do things that challenge you. You may even surprise yourself that you can handle more than you believe you can. Taking risks will help you live a more courageous life.

Is there something you have wanted to try but were too afraid to because it was either too hard or too scary?

How do you face a challenge that seems impossible to accomplish?

Are you always worried about failing and finding it difficult to move past that feeling? Who do you turn to for help when you are experiencing this worry?

What can you do to begin to live a more courageous life?

9

WHAT ARE YOUR TAKEAWAYS FROM PLATO?

In discovering Plato, you have started the process of learning to understand his philosophies. Doing so has required some skill and contemplation. It might seem that some of Plato's concepts are over your head. But by reflection, they are ideas you will be able to relate to and, hopefully, practice in your life.

So, why does Plato still matter today? He matters because he teaches us to lead a more virtuous and thoughtful life and grasp ideas that seem almost impossible to comprehend.

Plato wanted us to review our existence and question what is real and what is an illusion. Plato taught his students that every human should strive to be educated and be part of the world. He wanted them to seek truth and transform their lives. He wanted people to understand love in its complexities and how it affects us.

Plato was instrumental in bringing philosophy to the western world. He has influenced many people throughout the centuries with his logic and concepts. There is so much that you can learn from Plato's ideas. The main idea you might want to take away from Plato's teachings and philosophies are that knowledge is power. By learning and understanding this, you begin to develop that power. Hone it, nurture it, and it will take you on an extraordinary journey toward truth, conviction, and becoming a critical thinker.

BIBLIOGRAPHY

"Plato." *Wikipedia*, Wikimedia Foundation, 20 Mar. 2022, https://en.wikipedia.org/wiki/Plato

"Plato." *Encyclopædia Britannica*, Encyclopædia Britannica, Inc., https://www.britannica.com/biography/Plato.

Kraut, Richard. "Plato." *Stanford Encyclopedia of Philosophy*, Stanford University, 12 Feb. 2022, https://plato.stanford.edu/entries/plato/.

"Plato." *Biography.com*, A&E Networks Television, 25 May 2021, https://www.biography.com/scholar/plato.

Biography of Plato." *Plato*, 16 Nov. 2014, https://thegreatthinkers.org/plato/biography/.

Internet Encyclopedia of Philosophy, https://iep.utm.edu/plato/.

7, Nam-Ho Shin on September, and Thomas DeMichele on September 8. "Plato's Allegory of the Cave and Theory of the Forms Explained." *Fact / Myth*, 7 Oct. 2017, http://factmyth.com/platos-allegory-of-the-cave-and-theory-of-the-forms-explained/.

BIBLIOGRAPHY CONT.

Gray, Charles. "Can You Please Explain Plato's Theory of Forms in Simple Terms?" *Medium*, The Academy of You, 26 Apr. 2020, https://medium.com/the-academy-of-you/can-you-please-explain-platos-theory-of-forms-in-simple-terms-94fb454cb3fe

"Plato's Theory of Soul." *Wikipedia*, Wikimedia Foundation, 24 Jan. 2022, https://en.wikipedia.org/wiki/Plato%27s_theory_of_soul.

Philosophyfinds, /. "Plato's View on the Soul." *Philosophy and Ethics*, 18 June 2017, https://philosophyfinds.wordpress.com/2017/06/18/platos-view-on-the-soul/.

"Platonic Love." *Wikipedia*, Wikimedia Foundation, 19 Mar. 2022, https://en.wikipedia.org/wiki/Platonic_love

Kraut, Richard. "Plato on Love." *Oxford Handbooks Online*, 14 Aug. 2008, https://www.oxfordhandbooks.com/view/10.1093/oxfordhb/9780195182903.001.0001/oxfordhb-9780195182903-e-12.

Every heart sings a song, incomplete... – You are..., https://www.facebook.com/YourStoryteller2015/posts/every-heart-sings-a-song-incomplete-until-another-heart-whispers-back-platothe-m/1924672714385502/.

ILLUSTRATIONS

- Illustration 51750892 / Ancient Athens © Helen Vonallmen | Dreamstime.com

- Illustration 11840477 / Ancient © Johnfoto | Dreamstime.com

- Illustration 157014352 / Ancient © Mariobread | Dreamstime.com

- Photo 239442640 / Ancient © Volodymyr Polotovskyi | Dreamstime.com

- Illustration 107035413 © Arkadi Bojaršinov | Dreamstime.com

- Illustration 35566118 © Yuliia Brykova | Dreamstime.com

- Illustration 68251408 © Alain Lacroix | Dreamstime.com

- Illustration 39624119 © Kianlin | Dreamstime.com

- Illustration 168144725 © Julia Kutska | Dreamstime.com

- Illustration 94497093 © Pytyczech | Dreamstime.com

- Illustration 188240262 / Ancient © Matias Del Carmine | Dreamstime.com

- Illustration 239553486 © Elena Kuznetsova | Dreamstime.com

- Illustration 34480635 / Abstract © Jorgenmac | Dreamstime.com

- Illustration 163301587 © Patrick Guenette | Dreamstime.com

- Illustration 34278263 © Kakigori | Dreamstime.com

- Illustration 4086796 © Madartists | Dreamstime.com

- Illustration 83809904 © Selvam Raghupathy | Dreamstime.com

- Illustration 159529313 / Abstract © VectorMine | Dreamstime.com

- Illustration 196472869 / Abstract © Tatyana Antusenok | Dreamstime.com

- Illustration 120778707 / Abstract © Andegraund548 | Dreamstime.com

- Illustration 108598379 © Pavlo Syvak | Dreamstime.com

- Illustration 113331107 © Vladischern | Dreamstime.com

- Illustration 188399884 © Rodolphe Trider | Dreamstime.com

- Illustration 160233820 © Siedykholena | Dreamstime.com

- Illustration 149900210 © Makc76 | Dreamstime.com

- Illustration 94339002 © Rob3000 | Dreamstime.com

- Illustration 188237833 © Matias Del Carmine | Dreamstime.com

If You Enjoyed This Book, Please Leave a Review on Amazon.com, B&N, and Smashwords

Please Look for These Books in the Be a Great Thinker Series:

Book 1 – Introduction to Critical Thinking

Book 2 – Socrates – Man, Myth, Teacher

And Be Sure to Look for Other Books to be Released Soon in this Series!

ABOUT THE AUTHORS

Adrienne Roth and Matthew Roth are passionate about Philosophy and Critical Thinking. They have spent their lives exploring ways to quantify their arguments, questioning flawed ideas, and trying to bring people together through truth and reality. With this book series, they want to show young adults how to do the same in their lives.